Learning Decorativ

Shirring and Smocking

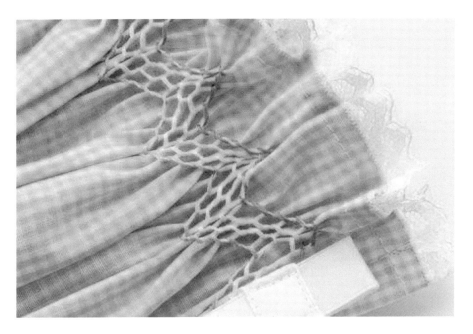

Dueep Jyot Singh

Learning Series

Mendon Cottage Books

JD-Biz Publishing

Download Free Books!

http://MendonCottageBooks.com

All Rights Reserved.

No part of this publication may be reproduced in any form or by any means, including scanning, photocopying, or otherwise without prior written permission from JD-Biz Corp Copyright © 2016

All Images Licensed by Fotolia and 123RF.

Disclaimer

The information is this book is provided for informational purposes only. The information is believed to be accurate as presented based on research by the author.

The author or publisher is not responsible for the use or safety of any procedure or treatment mentioned in this book. The author or publisher is not responsible for errors or omissions that may exist.

Our books are available at

1. Amazon.com
2. Barnes and Noble
3. Itunes
4. Kobo
5. Smashwords
6. Google Play Books

Download Free Books!

http://MendonCottageBooks.com

Table of Contents

Introduction

I was just moving around the local fabric market, when I noticed that a number of garments were embroidered with really attractive smocking stitches at the front and the back, the neck, yokes, pockets, sleeves, the bodices, necklines, bodices, cuffs, and even waists of a supposedly plain design and turn them into a thing of beauty.

Smocking is supposed to have originated in Europe somewhere in the medieval times, where buttons could not be afforded by the laborers to fasten the garment and fullness needed to be controlled. This was done with multiple rows of gathered fabric which was controlled over a wide area.

Nowadays, it is restricted to just babies and children's clothing primarily, even though you can use it on any garment which needs a bit of decorative embellishment.

Later on, smocking became a purely decorative design intended as a status symbol – the word originates from a peasants' shirt also known as a smock.

This was used extensively in almost every garment made by hand for laborers as well as for popular ordinary wear in the eighteenth as well as the nineteenth century.

Smocking at that time was done with crewel needles or embroidery needles with silken threads or cotton threads depending on the fabric. You will need about 3 times the initial width's material because of major part of it is going to be gathered up into folds, and stitched together. If you can gather the material, you can smock it.

Naturally, this was the best way in which clothes could be "gathered together" in the absence of elastic. The fabrics on which the stitches work best are lightweight and ones that can gather easily. These include gingham, muslin, crêpe de Chine, Cashmere, Swiss cotton, voile, Batiste, cottons, and handkerchief linens.

You can also say use crisp and soft crêpes, jerseys, and batises. You can also use – iron fabric because it is difficult to press any sort of smocking or sharing without flattening it.

When you are making up the pattern, you need to specify the area which needs to be shirred and smocked. Around 1880 you could get transfer dots which would be ironed on onto the pattern, but you could also make your own guide with a cardboard, and marking pencils. This is why smocking is also called gauging.

With an iron on transfer you are going to get dots placed evenly. You are going to turn the fabric over onto its wrong side. After that you are going to use a running stitch to pleat the fabric.

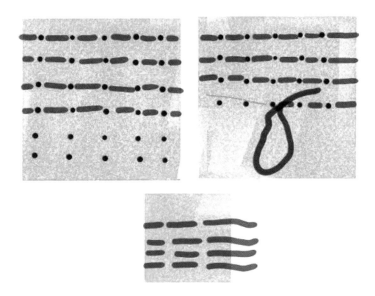

These running stitches are going to be removed easily, and they are just like basting stitches which are normally used to hold fabrics together before sewing. After that you can stabilize the bottom and the top of the work area with cable stitches.

Gathering

Before you start any shirring/smocking, you are going to need to know more about gathering. Gathering is the process of drawing a given amount of fabric into an already predetermined smaller area along one or more stitching lines to create soft and even folds.

Fabric is usually gathered to one half or one third of the original width. The effort can be soft or billowing or draped or crisp, depending on the fabric. This gathering is normally d one at cuffs, waistlines, and yokes.

Gathering is normally done after construction seams have been stitched, and pressed. Because gathers are based on the lengthwise grain, the row of stitching should run across the grain.

Stitch length for gathering is longer and tension is looser than usual. It is advisable to pretest both on a scrap of your fabric.

The suitable stitch lengths are going to vary from 2 – 4 mm or shorter for sheer or light fabrics. They are going to be longer for heavy and thick materials.

The shorter the stitch length is the more control you are going to have over the gathers no matter what the fabric is. **When you are gathering, it is the bobbin thread that is pulled.**

A looser upper tension is going to make it easier to slide the fabric along the thread. For heavy fabrics or extensive gathering, you can use an extra strength thread in the bobbin.

Start from the right side of the fabric. Stitch 2 parallel rows in seam allowance. One is going to be a thread width above the seam line. The other is going to be half an inch higher.

Leave a long thread end. Break stitching at the seams. That is because it is difficult to gather through 2 thicknesses.

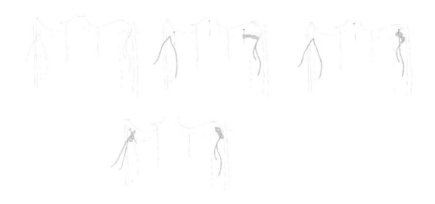

In the stitched edge to the corresponding straight edge with the right side together, match the notches, central lines, and seams.

Anchor the bobbin threads which are now facing you at one end twisting it in a figure 8 around a pin. This excess material is now ready to gather.

After that gently pull on the bobbin threads while with the other hand, you are sliding the fabric along the thread to create uniform gathers. When this first gathered section fits the adjoining edge, secure the thread ends by winding them in a tight figure 8 around a pin.

To draw up the un – gathered portion untie the bobbin threads and repeat the process from the other end. When the entire gathered edge matches the straight edge, fasten the thread end. Adjust the gathers uniformly and pin at frequent intervals to hold the folds in place.

Before seaming the gathered section, be sure that the machine is set to the stitch length suitable to the fabric and the tension is the balance. With the gathered side up, stitch the seam on the seam line, holding the fabric on either side of the needle so that the gathers are not stitched into little pleats.

Trim any seam allowances such as the side seams which are caught into the gathered seam. Press the seam as stitched in the seam allowances using just the tip of the iron. Seam finishes the edge with either a zigzag or an overhead stitch.

Open the garment section out flat and press the seam as it should go in the finished garment – towards the bodice, if it is the waist line seam, towards the shoulder, if it is the yoke seam, towards the end, if it is a cuff.

Again work with the tip of the iron, pressing the flat parts only taking care not to crease the folds.

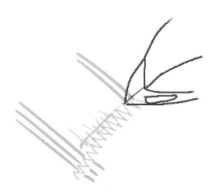

Using Cords for Gathers

This is going to be done with zigzag stitching over a thin and strong cord, especially when you are using a long strip or a bulky fiber which needs to be gathered.

Place the cord about 6 mm above the seam line. Use the widest zigzag stitch over the cord to hold it in place. Pull on the cord so that you can get the gathers.

Staying a Gathered Seam

You may often use a stay so that a gathered seam does not stretch or fray. You can also use this for reinforcing the seam. It also gives a professional look to the inside of a fabric, especially if you have gathered a curtain. These stays can be woven to seam binding, tape, or even Petersham ribbon.

With the gathered edge of the seam up, place the stay on the seam allowances so that one edge is right next to the permanent stitching.

Straight stitch close to the lower edge through all the thicknesses. Trim the seam allowances even with the top edge of the stay.

If the fabric frays readily, zigzag stitch the seam allowances to the stay. Press the seam and the stay in the proper direction. This is done by pressing the gathers by working the point of the iron into the gathers towards the seam.

Press from the wrong side of the fabric lifting the iron as you reach the seam. Do not press across the gathers. This will flatten them and cause them to go limp.

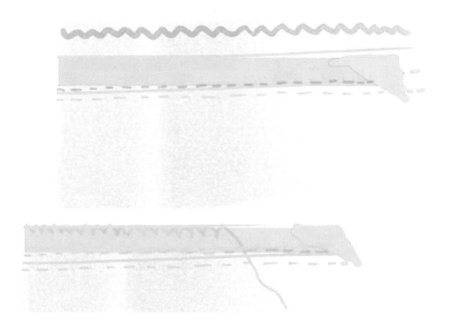

Do not trim the seam to be stayed until the tape has already been stitched on. Stitch along the top edge of the stay, if you think that the fabric is fragile.

Getting Started with Smocking

When you are getting ready to do the smocking, you are going to do the gathering first.

It is very easy to gather gingham because it already has a number of squares in the print. Stitches can be taken between the square lines between the squares. Or you can stitch into the center of the alternate squares.

You can start stitching at the edge of each square to produce tucks in alternate colors or stitch in the middle of the light squares so that you can get a dark panel.

A fabric with a small dot print or a small motif is going to look plain when it is gathered. These motifs are going to form a number of lines so that you can get a striped affect when you make the tucks.

These lines are also going to help keep the stitching straight.

You can also get a good affect, if you are looking at an all over subtle print when you are using a thread which is in subtle tone with the fabric's general print used for smocking.

Cable stitches and stem stitches are going to hold the tucks quite firmly. They are good outline stitches. They are usually worked along the top portion and edge. Apart from that, you can use a wave stitch to get a much looser and pleasing affect.

With 3 – 4 times the basic width of the fabric, for example, 6 – 8 inches, you are going to get 2 inches of smocking. The fabric is also going to depend upon the spacing between your dots and the design as well as the fabric thickness.

First measure the fabric before you have gathered it. Then do the gathering and then measure it again. After that, multiply the width so that you can get the shoulder and garment section of the garment. Along with that, allow a seam allowance of 15 mm x the length required.

Remember that when you are choosing the stitches depending on the final design you like. Remember that as you look at the tension in crocheting and knitting, you will have to look at the exact tension. It has to be even. If you are stitching with a tight tension pattern, you will need extra width for compensation in the fabric beforehand.

You can start by transferring a piece of dotted smocking transfer[1] cut large enough to fit across the fabric width. Transfer it on the wrong side of the fabric with the paper dot side placed downwards. Then press the dots with a hot iron on the fabric.

If you already have a print fabric with a number of dots on it in a regular pattern, you can use this as a guide. If the dots are too far apart, you can take an extra stitch between the dots.

The floss that you can use can be embroidery floss, knotted at one end. Start from the wrong side. Then insert the needle through to the right side at the first dot.

Bring the needle back to the wrong side. It should just be 1 mm in the front. Insert the needle again at the next Dot. Make a long stitch between the dots.

---

[1] http://www.ebay.com/itm/NEW-KNOTTS-SMOCKING-DOTS-IRON-ON-DOTS-TO-SMOCK-WITH-HEIRLOOM-NOTION-/321848921660?hash=item4aefb0ce3c:g:9bQAAMXQxzZRdYK2

You can look elsewhere for cheaper alternatives.

Continue along the row leaving a long thread tail. This is repeated across each row.

When you pull the entire thread dance together, evenly spacing the gathers and pleats until the panel is of the correct width along with seam. Tie off or knot the thread ends. Hold all the gathered threads together, after you have done this stitching and pull them up until the folds are close together. However, they should be still slightly loose. Tie the pair of thread ends securely together.

The stitching is going to be done by working across the fabric with a running stitch with a really sturdy thread, picking up a couple of threads at each Dot Mark. Complete all the rows in the same manner.

Also turn the gathered fabric over so that you find the tucks facing towards you. Ease the tucks until they are spaced evenly and straight.

Work a row of stem stitch along the top of the tucks. Use a guide so that the stitching is kept straight. You can open the tucks slightly for a guide as you stitch to keep level with a gathering thread.

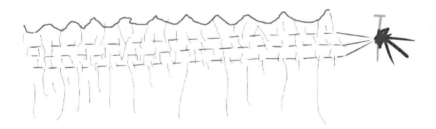

You can also twist the threads around a pin until they are ready to finish off. Remember to fasten off each row with back stitching on the wrong side.

Continue the stitching of all the bands of the smocking across the tucks. Count the tucks and place the diamonds and the zigzag patterns carefully. Choose a cable stitch or a stem stitch for the last row. You can also use the zigzag stitch like a Chevron stitch so that the gathers can be released properly.

Trellis and traditional diamonds are embellishing embroideries. You are going to use 3 strands of embroidery floss when you make these stitches.

You can also use up to 6 strands depending on how bold you want the final stitches to look.

Chevron stitch and wave stitch is also called a traditional diamond.

Traditional Diamond Stitch

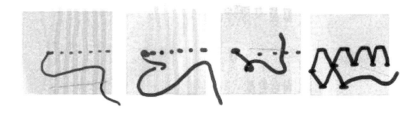

1. This is worked over 3 rows of running stitches. You are going to start at the left side, by bringing the needle up to the front of the work at the outer edge of the first pleat at the first running stitch row.

2. Insert the needle again into the right side of the second pleat. Bring back up between the first and second pleats. Pull the embroidery floss up to form a tight stitch.

3. Drop down to the second running stitch row. Take a stitch through the third pleat from right to left.

4. Now hold the thread below the needle and take the next stitch still on second running stitch row. This is going to be through the pleat 4, from right to left. Pull up again.

5. Returning to the first running stitch row you are going to take the stitch from the pleat 5, right to left, keeping the embroidery floss **below the needle.**

Now move the embroidery floss to the above needle and take a stitch in 6 again working from right to left. Pull up the floss again.

Continue across the pleats working with the top 2 running stitch rows. Now make a diamond shape by starting at the third running stitch row, first pleat and continue to stitch – 1 – 5 – working over the second and third running stitch rows. Note that on the center row, they are going to be 2 stitches formed at each pleat.

Different Types of Stitches

Cable Stitch

This is made in double rows tightly, so that you can join alternating gather columns. For this you are going to pick up every tuck in turn keeping the needle completely straight.

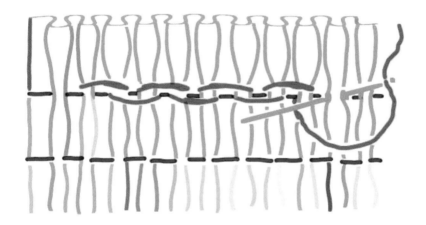

Honeycomb stitch and Surface Honeycomb

Honeycomb

This starts at the top left part. This is a variant of the cable stitch of medium density. This is going to provide more spacing between 2 gathers in double stitches. They are going to be made on gather sets. The diagonal stitch which intervenes is going to be hidden on the fabric's reverse side.

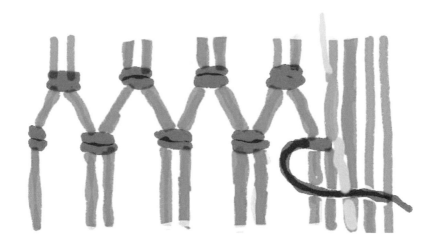

Surface Honeycomb

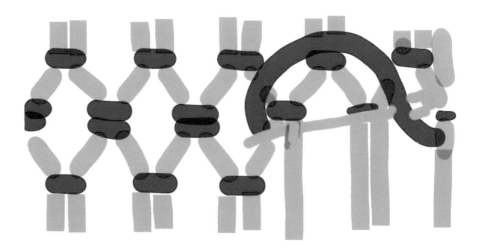

The surface honeycomb is going to start at the top left portion. This is going to stitch through 2 tucks and bringing the needle out between them. After that you are going to take a stitch below through the same tuck then stitch over 2 tucks bringing the needle out in the middle as before.

You are going to use a variation of the wave and the honeycomb so that you can see the diagonal visibly. However, this is going to be done on just one gather. You are not going to be using one gather and one space here.

Outline back stitch Also Known As Stem Stitch

You are going to take back stitches through each tuck with the thread kept below the needle. This is a tight stem stitch with low flexibility. This gathers 2 columns at the same time sloping downwards and in overlapping and single rows.

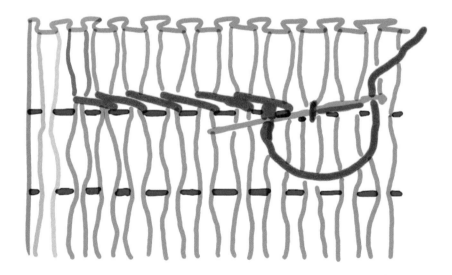

A front outline stitch is going to be when the needle slopes upwards.

Chevron Stitch

This is similar to surface honeycomb stitch. However, the diagonal thread is going to go across two tucks rather than one tuck.

Wave Stitch

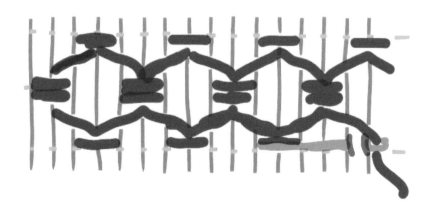

You can do this stitch by starting in the middle on the left. Take a stitch through 2 tucks. Bring the needle out between them. Then stitch over the next 2 tucks continuing up in a diagonal. Bring the needle out below the stitches to work back down. This uses both loose diagonals as well as tight horizontals.

Trellis stitch

This uses both stem stitches as well as outline stitches so that you get a diamond shaped pattern.

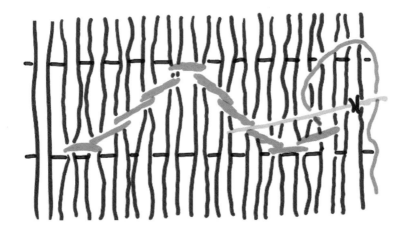

Just like the wave stitch, [traditional diamond stitch, given below] you are going to bring the embroidery thread up at the left edge of first pleat, but at the second running stitch row.

Now take a stitch diagonally through the second pleat so that the needle comes up just above the second row, keeping the floss below the needle.

Take the next stitch in the third pleat, again working from right coming down slightly higher diagonally on the left. Repeat for pleat number 4 and 5 so that pleat 5 finishes at the first running stitch row.

Repeat this in reverse, over the next 6 rows going down to the second running stitch. Continue this all across the pleats.

Again, start at the second running stitch row and work diagonally down over the pleats and then back to the second row over the next 5 pleats. Continue across all the pleats to finish.

Measuring for Smocking

If you want to complete an entire front of a bodice done in smocking measure the width of your pattern at the widest part. Now cut a straight piece of the dress fabric 3 times the width and 2 inches longer than the pattern.

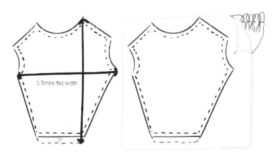 

Cut the smocking guide out of heavy paper the same size as the bodice pattern + 2 inches for seams and taking up of the smocking.

Mark the fabric for the smocking design. If you are not using any commercial transfer pattern, you can work out the design on your own self, and mark it accordingly.

Gather the fabric along the first row of dots to fit the top edge of the smocking guide. Baste the fabric to the guide along this edge.

Now baste the side edges as well as the center of the fabric to the guide so that it is kept secure until the smocking has been finished.

Remember that you need to do the smocking first before you finish tailoring a garment. A garment which has already been tailored and then you do the smocking on it means that you have gathered the already measured fabric which was cut out for the pattern.

When the smocking is finished, remove it from the smocking guide and do a light seam press upon it **before you cut out the bodice.**

Pin the top row of the shirring to the ironing board. Hold the iron just above the fabric surface so that the seam can penetrate. At the same time you are going to be stretching the smocking from the bottom, gently. This is going to form even pleats.

Now cut the bodice pattern again from Brown paper or on the cloth, like muslin – I am using red smocked Muslin here – but *remove all of the seam allowances* so you have a copy of the finished size.

Lay this over the smocking. *Make sure to line up the center of the bodice pattern with the center of the smocking.*

Also, be sure that the lower edge of the bodice is along the lower row of the smocking. Now mark around the neck, armhole, shoulder, waistline, and side seam on the smocking. Mark with a basting thread and remove the pattern. After that, sew around the marked lines by machine.

Now mark a 5/8 inch seam allowance outside the stitching line and cut out the smocking bodice along this line.

Now you can make up the dress using the smocking piece to form the front bodice. It is not necessary to sew bodice darts into smocking because it is already tight. You can, however, ease it slightly at the waist line if you want.

If the smocking is to be used under a yoke, you are going to measure the width of the bodice where it joins the yoke and cut the fabric 2 ½ – 3 times this width. Follow the same procedure for smocking and cutting as you do for the whole bodice.

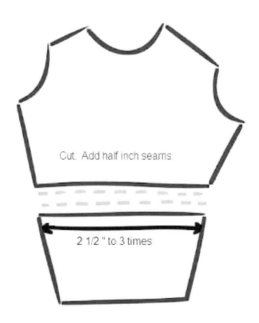

Cut. Add half inch seams

2 1/2 " to 3 times

Helpful Tips

Here are some easy helpful tips, which are going to facilitate your smocking project.

Naturally, the easiest way to mark your fabric for smocking is with a transfer pattern which you can get from a number of pattern companies.

However, if you need only straight blocks of dots for honeycomb or cable smocking you can do this by machine.

Mark the lines for the dots on the wrong side of the fabric with tailors chalk. Also mark a line down the left side of the fabric. Baste the fabric to a piece of dressmakers carbon. The right side of the fabric should be against the carbon side.

Now remove the thread from the sewing machine. Adjust the stitch to the largest size, about 3/16th inch on most machines or depending on the machine make. Stitch along the chalk marks on the wrong side of the fabric with the carbon between the fabric and the sewing machine.

Make sure that the pressure on the pressure foot is not very heavy. If the pressure is correct, you are going to get a really clean and clear dot pattern without any smudging of carbon.

Start each row of stitching by putting the needle down through the vertical chalk line. This is going to align the rows of dots correctly.

Gauging

You can also try advanced gathering which is known as gauging to make the dots.

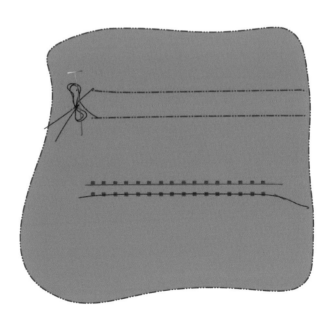

This is done by making small stitches under the dots, as you are going to see in the diagram given above. Making small stitches under the dots as shown, sew along each row. Leave one end loose – draw up 2 rows at a time to the desired width. Dots are going to appear at the tops of the folds to indicate the smocking stitch points.

If you are making a pattern for a more complicated banding design, workout the design on graph paper beforehand. You can use corners of the squares on the papers for dots.

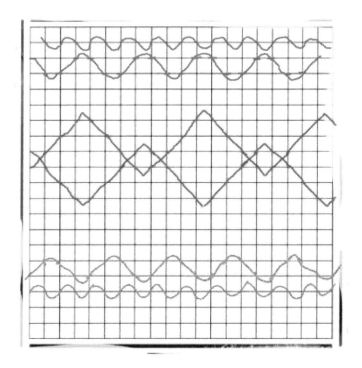

After the smocking has been finished, you can fill in other colors by working in by doing fill-in rows. This is done by either filling in white spaces above or below the stitch with the same stitch, but done in a contrasting color. Take the stitches in pleats formed by the original smocking row.

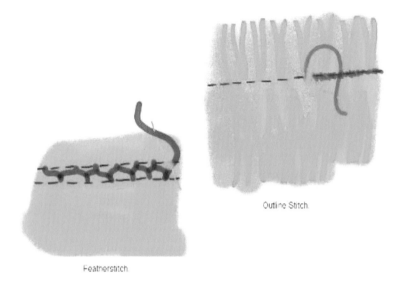

Outline Stitch.

Featherstitch

Here is another good embroidery choice – featherstitching, which is a stitch used in ordinary embroidery.

You can also use another embroidery stitch, which looks a bit like wave stitch. Bring the needle to the right side through the top line of the shirring. Take stitch to the right with thread above the needle.

Bring the needle out half way back to the point where the thread comes to the right side. Make small stitches on the lower line of the shirring to the right of the stitch on the top row.

Then take the stitch to the right with the thread below the needle.

Now bring the needle out at the end of the down stroke from the top row. Continue working towards the right on the top row then on the lower row.

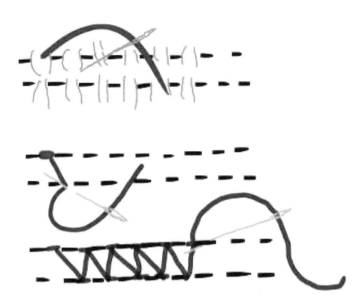

Machine Smocking Also Known As Shirring

You can get a similar effect to hand smocking with shirring thread or even shirring elastic either in the bobbin or by couching the zigzag stitches.

You can also get the effect of smocking by using embroidery over ordinary machine shirring. You are going to sew rows of shirring by machine at a point where you want the smocking affect.

Ease the shirring to size. Then you can use the same outline stitch you used for regular smocking.

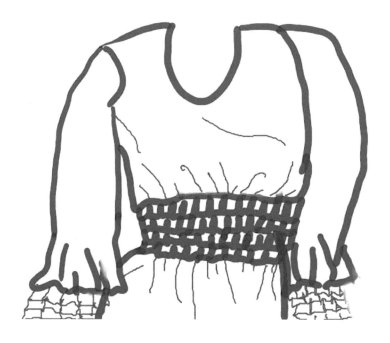

When you contrast it to gathering in which the fullness is controlled within just one seam the fullness in shirring is controlled over a wider area.

Just like smocking, lightweight fabrics are also the best fabric for this, and also more appropriate when the fabric is crisp and soft. Jerseys, crêpes, and even voiles are excellent choices for shirring with a machine.

You can also use non iron fabrics, because it is difficult to press the shirring without it getting flattened. This pattern needs to specify the area that needs to be shirred which can either range from a small part such as a cuff or an entire bodice section.

The shirring rows have to be parallel straight and equidistant. They can be as close together as 6 mm or as far apart as 2 – 3 cm, depending on your preference or the specifications of the pattern.

Width to be shirred is determined by the pattern.

Used 2 threads through one needle, or use a thicker thread on the bobbin and work with the right side facing down.

Stitch parallel rows of decorative stitching across the width as you are going to do with hand stitching.

Stitch further parallel zigzag rows between the decorative rows, couching the shirring elastic in place. Turn up the elastic until the panel is of the desired width.

You can also use a strong thread and a long stitch to make 3 or more parallel rows of stitching. Keep the lines evenly spaced by using the narrow or the wide side of the presser foot as your guide.

Bring the ends of all the threads together and pull at the same time. This will help in the sliding of the shirring along the threads to distribute the fullness evenly. To fasten, pull each top thread to the wrong side and tie to its own bobbin thread.

Tips for Machine Shirring

When you are going to start shirring on, let us say a garment, you will need to mark the pattern with 2 lines showing exactly where it goes. Mark the shirring the way you mark notches. That means you are going to slash the seam for about ¼ inches at either end of the gathered lines.

After you have enlarged the stitch on the machine, loosen the upper tension. Sew 2 rows of stitching about ¼ inches apart.

Mark the first row on the seam allowance line. As you begin your shirring, you are going to sew between the slashes on the right side of the fabric.

Shirr by easing the fabric along on the bobbin thread. If the shirring is very full, with a lot of fabric to be eased in, you can use a nylon thread in the bobbin. That is because it is stronger and less likely to break as you do the shirring.

You are going to use at least 2 rows of stitching when you gather, so your fabric does not roll and is easier to handle. The advantage of gathering by machine is that it can be done really quickly. Apart from that, you are going to get the gathers in even folds.

Another tip – professionals normally use the largest stitch on the machine, but if you are using soft and sheer fabrics such as chiffon, the gathers are going to be finer if you use a smaller machine stitch.

You can gauge the size of the stitch by the weight and the texture of the fabric that you are using.

Sometimes the style of the pattern may ask for a number of rows of gathers. You can sew as many rows as you like by machine. When you are gathering, the trick is to ease all the rows on the bobbin threads at once.

Couching

This is normally done by using decorative thread in the bobbin and is worked with the wrong side uppermost.

Couch elastic down by using wide zigzag stitches, stitching over but not through the elastic.

Pull up the elastic and adjust the gathers on the right side before steam pressing.

http://www.craftsy.com/blog/2014/09/sewing-machine-embroidery/

This is another extra stitch method which you can do with your sewing machine.

Fagotting

This is another way in which you can produce a really decorative finish to the fabric. In this method, you are going to be joining 2 pieces of fabric with a decorative stitch. That means you are leaving a space between 2 fabric edges.

Neaten the raw edges of the fabric pieces which you need to join. After that, turn the neaten edges to the wrong side. – 13 mm. [1/4 inches].

Now select a favorite decorative stitch on your sewing machine that is going to incorporate a zigzag action.

Then pin a soluble stabilizer underneath the 2 fabric pieces while keeping them evenly spaced apart. They should not be more than 3 mm stitch so that the stitches catch the folded fabric edges on both the sides by at least half a millimeter.

Then wash away the stabilizer.

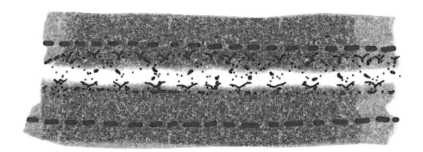

Finishing the Smocking

Once you have completed the smocking, pin it with the embroidered side down on the ironing board.

Hold a steam iron above the tucks. The folds and the stitches are going to be set by the steam. You can also do this by working on a flat surface with the fabric right side up smoothing the pleats until they are evenly spaced and then hover a steam iron above the pleats, so that you can do a steam press. Do not let the iron rest on the fabric.

Allow the piece to dry. Now untie the thread ends and pull out each of the gathered threads.

Here is one tip – make sure that the floss is held above the needle when you are moving down a row and below the needle when you are moving up a row.

This smocking can also be finished with hand-embroidered surface stitches worked from the right side. The running stitches creating the pleats are going to be used as stitching guidelines.

Conclusion

This book has given you a bit of knowledge about an interesting embroidery style, with a number of stitches to make up a really attractive a really attractive surface on a garment.

So enjoy smocking on your fabric before stitching it and wear it with pride.

Here are some more interesting URLs, if you are ready to try a project. –

Try Canadian smocking.

https://www.youtube.com/watch?v=EVH-kC4Rw6A

https://www.youtube.com/watch?v=AYXmLfZnA0g

Live Long and Prosper!

Author Bio

Dueep Jyot Singh is a Management and IT Professional who managed to gather Postgraduate qualifications in Management and English and Degrees in Science, French and Education while pursuing different enjoyable career options like being an hospital administrator, IT,SEO and HRD Database Manager/ trainer, movie , radio and TV scriptwriter, theatre artiste and public speaker, lecturer in French, Marketing and Advertising, ex-Editor of Hearts On Fire (now known as Solstice) Books Missouri USA, advice columnist and cartoonist, publisher and Aviation School trainer, ex-moderator on Medico.in, banker, student councilor ,travelogue writer … among other things!

One fine morning, she decided that she had enough of killing herself by Degrees and went back to her first love -- writing. It's more enjoyable! She already has 48 published academic and 14 fiction- in- different- genre books under her belt.

When she is not designing websites or making Graphic design illustrations for clients , she is browsing through old bookshops hunting for treasures, of which she has an enviable collection – including R.L. Stevenson, O.Henry, Dornford Yates, Maurice Walsh, De Maupassant, Victor Hugo, Sapper, C.N. Williamson, "Bartimeus" and the crown of her collection- Dickens "The Old Curiosity Shop," and "Martin Chuzzlewit" and so on… Just call her "Renaissance Woman" - collecting herbal remedies, acting like Universal Helping Hand/Agony Aunt, or escaping to her dear mountains for a bit of exploring, collecting herbs and plants, and trekking.

Check out some of the other JD-Biz Publishing books

Gardening Series on Amazon

Download Free Books!

http://MendonCottageBooks.com

Health Learning Series

Country Life Books

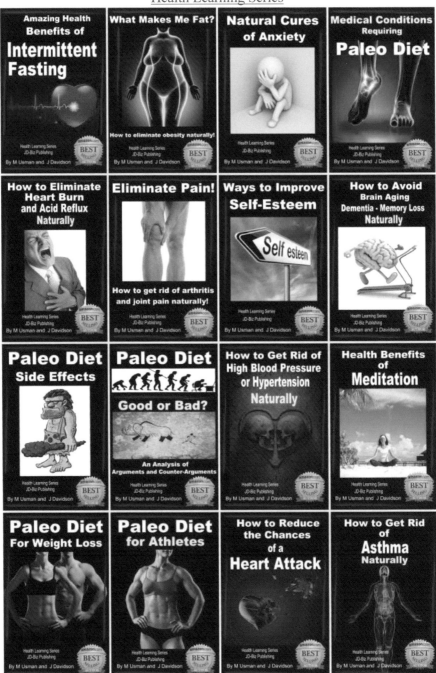

Amazing Animal Book Series

Learn To Draw Series

How to Build and Plan Books

Entrepreneur Book Series

Our books are available at

1. Amazon.com

2. Barnes and Noble

3. Itunes

4. Kobo

5. Smashwords

6. Google Play Books

Download Free Books!

http://MendonCottageBooks.com

Publisher

JD-Biz Corp

P O Box 374

Mendon, Utah 84325

http://www.jd-biz.com/

CPSIA information can be obtained at www.ICGtesting.com
Printed in the USA
BVIW12n1807210816
459717BV00008B/52